Lerner SPORTS

SPORTS ALL-STARS

LAMAR JACKSON

Jon M. Fishman

Lerner Publications ◆ Minneapolis

Lerner Publications Company
An imprint of Lerner Publishing Group, Inc.
241 First Avenue North
Minneapolis, MN 55401 USA

For reading levels and more information, look up this title at www.lernerbooks.com.

Main body text set in Albany Std 22. Typeface provided by Agfa.

Editor: Brianna Kaiser

Library of Congress Cataloging-in-Publication Data

Names: Fishman, Jon M., author.
Title: Lamar Jackson / Jon M. Fishman.
Description: Minneapolis : Lerner Publications, [2021] | Series: Sports all-stars (Lerner sports) | Includes bibliographical references and index. | Audience: Ages 7–11 | Audience: Grades 2–3 | Summary: "Baltimore Ravens quarterback Lamar Jackson is a star on the field. Readers will devour the life story of this athlete with the golden throwing arm and cheetah-like speed!"— Provided by publisher.
Identifiers: LCCN 2020003613 (print) | LCCN 2020003614 (ebook) | ISBN 9781541598966 (library binding) | ISBN 9781728413990 (paperback) | ISBN 9781728401041 (ebook)
Subjects: LCSH: Jackson, Lamar, 1997– —Juvenile literature. | Quarterbacks (Football)—United States—Biography—Juvenile literature. | Baltimore Ravens (Football team)—Juvenile literature.
Classification: LCC GV939.J29 F57 2021 (print) | LCC GV939.J29 (ebook) | DDC 796.332092 [B]—dc23

LC record available at https://lccn.loc.gov/2020003613
LC ebook record available at https://lccn.loc.gov/2020003614

Manufactured in the United States of America
1-48092-48745-4/2/2020

CONTENTS

Lamar Jackson dodges New York Jets defenders.

Baltimore Ravens quarterback Lamar Jackson faked a hand off to his running back. Gripping the ball in both hands, Jackson sprinted to his right. He streaked five yards up the field before a group of New York Jets players knocked him to the ground.

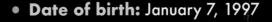

- **Date of birth:** January 7, 1997

- **Position:** quarterback

- **League:** National Football League (NFL)

- **Professional highlights:** chosen with the last pick in the first round of the 2018 NFL Draft; led Baltimore to the best record in the NFL in 2019; became the first player to pass for 3,000 yards and rush for 1,000 yards in a season

- **Personal highlights:** grew up in southern Florida; won the 2016 **Heisman Trophy**; dressed up as Harry Potter for a charity Halloween party

The Jets and Ravens were playing in Baltimore, Maryland, on December 12, 2019. The five-yard gain gave Jackson almost 1,050 rushing yards for the year. No other quarterback in NFL history had ever gained so many yards in a season.

To beat Baltimore, New York had to stop Jackson on the ground and in the air. But they couldn't keep up with him. Later in the first quarter, Jackson tossed a five-yard touchdown pass to Miles Boykin. The score gave the Ravens a 13–0 lead.

Jackson rushes past a reaching Jets defender.

Jackson passes the ball to an open receiver.

In the third quarter, Jackson threw two long touchdowns. Then he passed for a 10-yard score in the fourth quarter. He finished the game with five touchdowns and almost 300 combined passing and rushing yards. The Ravens crushed the Jets, 42–21.

The win gave Baltimore a 12–2 record, the best in the NFL. It also made them **division** champions. The Ravens celebrated in the locker room, but they didn't get too excited. Winning the division was just one step in a long journey for Jackson and his teammates. Their goal was the Super Bowl.

NATURAL-BORN
PASSER

Jackson looks to pass for the Louisville Cardinals.

Lamar Jackson grew up in Pompano Beach, Florida, with his brother and two sisters. Southern Florida is a **hotbed** for football players. But as a young kid, Lamar didn't care much about the sport.

Pompano Beach, Florida

In 2005, when Lamar was eight years old, his father had a heart attack and died. Lamar's mother, Felicia Jones, became a single parent to her four children. She did everything for them, from shopping to playing tackle football in the yard.

That year Jones enrolled Lamar in a youth football league. At first, he wasn't excited about playing. But he was the fastest player on the field, and he liked scoring touchdowns. He decided football was pretty fun after all.

Lamar grew to love playing quarterback. His large hands helped him grip the ball and throw quick, accurate

Jackson practices with the
Boynton Beach Tigers.

passes. With his mother supporting and pushing him, he worked to get better. In 2013, he became the **varsity** quarterback at Boynton Beach Community High School.

Lamar became a star at Boynton Beach. He showed off his skill against Miami Central, which was the third-ranked high school team in the United States at the time. In the game, he had 417 combined passing and rushing yards. Boynton Beach lost, but Lamar's performance drew attention from top college coaches around the country.

Lamar had enough talent to play college football, but some coaches weren't sure what position he should play. They thought he was a better runner than a thrower.

Some teams even thought he should play defense.

   Lamar wanted to play quarterback, and Jones supported her son's wish. Bobby Petrino, then the head football coach at the University of Louisville, told the family that Lamar would play only quarterback for his team. That was good enough for Lamar and Jones. In 2015, he joined the Louisville Cardinals.

Jackson throws a pass for the Cardinals in 2015.

Petrino kept his promise. As a freshman, Jackson played 12 games as quarterback. Then, in 2016, he had one of the best seasons in college football history. He threw 30 touchdowns and just nine **interceptions**. He also rushed for 1,571 yards. That year Jackson won the Heisman Trophy as the best player in college football. He was the youngest Heisman winner ever. "I'm extremely proud to represent this class and the University of Louisville with their first Heisman Trophy," he said.

Jackson and his mom, Felicia Jones, pose with the Heisman Trophy in 2016.

Jackson holds up a Baltimore Ravens jersey during the 2018 NFL Draft.

In 2017, Jackson returned to Louisville for his junior season. He threw 27 touchdown passes and rushed for 1,601 yards. He felt ready to move on and entered the 2018 NFL Draft. But some **scouts** still thought Jackson was a better runner than a passer. He waited as teams chose other quarterbacks. Finally, with the last pick in the first round of the draft, Baltimore chose Jackson.

Jackson carries the ball down the field.

Jackson's football skills have always been special. As a kid, he threw the ball farther than his teammates could throw. He leaped, spun, and twisted away from defenders as he raced to the **end zone**. When his mother saw him play, she was impressed. Jones created a plan to turn Jackson into a football superstar.

Jackson would run back and forth across a bridge to train.

Six days a week, Jones and Jackson worked out and practiced. Saturday was their only day off. It was easy to convince Jackson to work hard. "I did it because I wanted to be great," he said.

Most days, they ran back and forth across a bridge in Pompano Beach. Then Jones, Jackson, and his younger brother, Jamar, put on football pads and practiced in the yard. They did the same drills Jackson learned from his coaches. They even tackled one another.

As Jackson got older, the workouts with his mother got tougher. Lying on his back with a heavy exercise ball in his hands, Jackson would twist back and forth for three minutes. Then, with his stomach muscles burning, he would stand and throw the ball to Jones. They also did **squats** and other moves to strengthen Jackson's arms and legs.

In college, Jackson became even more dedicated to exercise. He set an example for his teammates by beginning his workouts at six in the morning. He grew bigger and stronger, and soon he could **bench-press** almost 300 pounds (136 kg).

For Jackson, a trip to the beach was no time to rest. He ran on the sand. Then Jackson practiced football moves in the ocean.

Growing up, Jackson practiced throwing the ball with his mom.

In the NFL, Jackson works harder than ever to stay strong and fast.

By the time Jackson reached the NFL, he weighed 212 pounds (96 kg). He had never been in better shape, but he wanted to get stronger. With more muscle, he could break free from more tackles during games. After his first year, Jackson spent the off-season working out. When the 2019 season began, he had gained almost 10 pounds (4.5 kg) of muscle.

Jackson shows off his Heisman Trophy.

Jackson doesn't play football for money or fame. His mother taught him to play the game and not worry about anything else. But in 2016, as he played his Heisman Trophy–winning season at Louisville, he couldn't avoid the spotlight.

In September, he appeared on the cover of *Sports Illustrated* magazine. He had just scored 18 touchdowns in Louisville's first three games. The headline read, "What Just Happened? Lamar Jackson Arrived, That's What." At Boynton Beach Community High School, members of the Art Department enlarged the magazine cover and made posters. They hung the posters in the principal's office and in the lobby of the school auditorium. At a park where Jackson played as a kid,

Jackson (*right*) and other football players celebrate at the 2016 Heisman Trophy presentation.

Jackson signs a jersey for a fan.

fans hung a sign in honor of the quarterback: "Welcome to the city of Pompano Beach, home of the 2016 Heisman Trophy Winner."

With the Ravens, Jackson is more popular than ever. At home games, the stands are full of fans wearing Jackson jerseys. Ticket sales are up, and Jackson gets tons of requests for autographs and interviews.

children throughout the school year.

In 2019, Jackson attended a Halloween party. The event raised money to help kids at risk of bullying and other dangers. Partygoers ate, danced, and voted in a costume contest. Jackson dressed up as the famous wizard Harry Potter.

Blessings in a Backpack provides food for children throughout the school year.

The Ravens practice at the Under Armour Performance Center in Owings Mills, Maryland.

Despite the attention, Jackson lives a quiet life. In 2018, his family bought a home in Owings Mills, Maryland, where he lives with his mom and siblings. The big house has a pool and a three-car garage. But more important, it's just a few miles from the Ravens practice field. Jackson just wants to play football.

RAVEN KING

Jackson leaps with the ball before being tackled.

When Jackson joined the Ravens in 2018, he became the backup to starting quarterback Joe Flacco. Flacco had been the team's starter since 2008. In 2013, he won the Super Bowl Most Valuable Player (MVP) award as Baltimore beat the San Francisco 49ers to win the championship.

Ravens coaches were happy with Flacco. But in a game in November 2018, the **veteran** quarterback injured his hip. Jackson took over, and the team won three of the next four games. When Flacco was healthy again about a month later, the coaches kept Jackson in the game.

Quarterback Joe Flacco runs with the ball in 2018.

The Ravens got their nickname from a famous poem. In the mid–19th century, Edgar Allan Poe wrote "The Raven" while living in Baltimore.

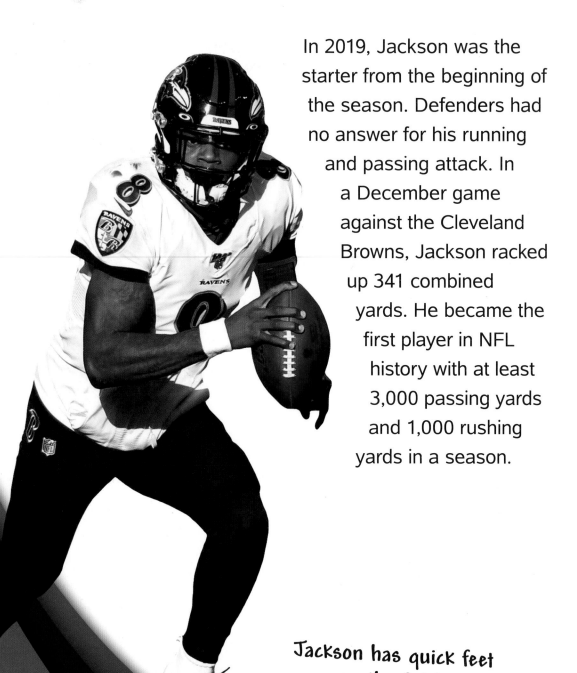

In 2019, Jackson was the starter from the beginning of the season. Defenders had no answer for his running and passing attack. In a December game against the Cleveland Browns, Jackson racked up 341 combined yards. He became the first player in NFL history with at least 3,000 passing yards and 1,000 rushing yards in a season.

Jackson has quick feet on the field.

Jackson celebrates with teammate Matt Skura in 2019.

It was a great year for Jackson. He won his first NFL MVP award, and Baltimore won 14 games, the most in the NFL. But in their first playoff game, they lost to the Tennessee Titans. Jackson's talent and hard work will soon carry the Ravens deeper into the playoffs. "We can only get better," Jackson said. "It's only up from here."

All-Star Stats

When Lamar Jackson entered the NFL, many fans still thought he was a better runner than a passer. In 2019, he proved them wrong. Take a look at where Jackson ranked in NFL passing touchdowns for the season.

Player	Team	Passing touchdowns in 2019
1. Lamar Jackson	Baltimore Ravens	36
2. Jameis Winston	Tampa Bay Buccaneers	33
3. Russell Wilson	Seattle Seahawks	31
4. Dak Prescott	Dallas Cowboys	30
5. Carson Wentz	Philadelphia Eagles	27
6. Jimmy Garoppolo	San Francisco 49ers	27
7. Drew Brees	New Orleans Saints	27

Glossary

bench-press: to lift a weight by extending the arms upward while lying on a bench

division: a group of teams in the NFL. Each division winner goes to the playoffs.

end zone: the area at each end of a football field marked by the end line, the goal line, and the sidelines

Heisman Trophy: an annual award given to college football's most outstanding player

hotbed: a place that favors rapid growth

interceptions: passes caught by the opposing team that result in a change of possession

scouts: people who judge the skills of athletes

squats: exercises in which a standing person lowers to a position in which the knees are deeply bent and then rises

varsity: the top team at a school

veteran: a player with a lot of experience

12 Steve Jones, "Text of Lamar Jackson's Heisman Speech," *Louisville Courier Journal,* December 10, 2016, https://www.courier-journal.com/story/sports/college/louisville/2016/12/10/full-text-lamar-jackson-heisman-speech/95289342/.

15 Andrea Adelson, "The Driving Force behind Lamar Jackson's Success Is His First Trainer—His Mom," ESPN, November 1, 2016, https://www.espn.com/college-football/story/_/id/17949555/louisville-cardinals-quarterback-lamar-jackson-first-trainer-was-mother.

20 "What Just Happened? Lamar Jackson Arrived, That's What," *Sports Illustrated,* accessed January 12, 2020, https://www.sicovers.com/what-just-happened-lamar-jackson-arrived-thats-what-2016-september-26.

21 Childs Walker, "How Lamar Jackson Used More Than Talent to Rise from the Fields of South Florida: 'He Continued to Work,'" *Baltimore Sun,* November 25, 2019, https://www.baltimoresun.com/sports/ravens/bs-sp-ravens-lamar-jackson-origins-20191126-cnqpz2aalfauni6fofhlxvom2y-story.html.

27 Jamison Hensley, "Lamar Jackson Struggles as Top-Seeded Ravens Shocked by Titans," ESPN, January 11, 2020, https://www.espn.com/nfl/story/_/id/28467215/lamar-jackson-struggles-top-seeded-ravens-shocked-titans.

Further Information

Baltimore Ravens
https://www.baltimoreravens.com/

Lamar Jackson—Heisman
https://www.heisman.com/heisman-winners/lamar-jackson/

Levit, Joe. *Football's G.O.A.T.: Jim Brown, Tom Brady, and More*. Minneapolis: Lerner Publications, 2020.

Monson, James. *Behind the Scenes Football*. Minneapolis: Lerner Publications, 2020.

Sports Illustrated Kids
https://www.sikids.com/football

Whiting, Jim. *Baltimore Ravens*. Mankato, MN: Creative Education, 2019.

Index

Photo Acknowledgments

Image credits: Mark Goldman/Icon Sportswire/Getty Images, pp. 4, 5; Patrick Smith/Getty Images, pp. 6, 7, 24; Andy Lyons/Getty Images, pp. 8, 11; PAG Photos and Designs/Shutterstock.com, p. 9; © Madeline Gray/The Palm Beach Post/ZUMAPRESS.com/Alamy Stock Photo, p. 10; Michael Reaves/Getty Images, p. 12; Andrew Dieb/Icon Sportswire/Getty Images, p. 13; Harry How/Getty Images, p. 14; Michael Ross Kupillas/Shutterstock.com, p. 15; Nick Cammett/Diamond Images/Getty Images, pp. 17, 18, 26; Todd Van Emst - Pool/Getty Images, p. 19; Michael Reaves/Getty Images, p. 20; Doug Murray/Icon Sportswire/Getty Images, p. 21; Don Juan Moore/Vera Bradley/Getty Images, p. 22; Rob Carr/Getty Images, p. 23; Streeter Lecka/Getty Images, p. 25; Karl Merton Ferron/Baltimore Sun/Tribune News Service/Getty Images, p. 27.

Cover image: Jayne Kamin-Oncea/Getty Images.